the
hundredth
monkey

ken keyes, jr.

VISION BOOKS

This book is not copyrighted.

You are asked to reproduce it in whole or in part, to distribute it with or without charge, in as many languages as possible, to as many people as possible.

The rapid alerting of all humankind to nuclear realities is supremely urgent. If we are wiped out by nuclear destruction in the next few years, how important are the things we are doing today?

First edition, January, 1982	100,000
Second edition, May, 1982	100,000
Third edition, October, 1982	100,000

Library of Congress Catalog Card No.
81-70978

VISION BOOKS
790 Commercial Avenue
Coos Bay, Oregon 97420

This book
is dedicated
to the Dinosaurs,
who mutely warn us
that a species
which cannot adapt
to changing conditions
will become
extinct.

Other Vital Books by
Ken Keyes, Jr.

**How to Enjoy Your Life
in Spite of It All**

**A Conscious Person's Guide
to Relationships**

Prescriptions for Happiness

Handbook to Higher Consciousness

Taming Your Mind

**How to Make Your Life Work or
Why Aren't You Happy?**
(Tolly Burkan, coauthor)

These are available from bookstores
or by mail order from

VISION BOOKS
790 Commercial Avenue
Coos Bay, Oregon 97420

FOREWORD

Two events converged on me this summer. They supplemented each other and gave me the inspiration and added push I needed. They made me respond to the urgency I had felt brewing in me for some time to express my concern about the worldwide danger of nuclear weapons.

The first event was my viewing the videotape "The Last Epidemic," taken at a symposium held in November, 1980 on the unacceptability of nuclear weapons for human health. I was deeply impressed by the physicians and scientists who brought their knowledge and eloquence to that meeting. Their stature and level of experience, insight and courage left no doubt in my mind that my priorities had to be rearranged. I had to add my voice and speak out now!

The second experience was my exposure to the Hundredth Monkey Phenomenon, which I learned about in talks by Marilyn Ferguson and Carl Rogers. This phenomenon shows that when enough of us are aware of something, all of us become aware of it.

That concept confirmed my own intuitive trust in the basic tenet of my work—that the appreciation and love we have for ourselves and others creates an expanding energy field that becomes a growing power in the world. This radical new support gives me the counterbalance of hope to off-set the doomsday story of nuclear destruction.

There is no need to feel helpless or get paralyzed by hopelessness. We know we have the power to make changes if we can join together and raise our voices in unison. There is more power in numbers than we ever hoped to dream about! I call for us to let our numbers grow exponentially as we all take it on ourselves to spread these messages.

We are the bearers of a new vision. We can dispel the old destructive myths and replace them with the life-enriching truths that are essential to continued life on our planet.

St. Mary, Kentucky   Ken Keyes, Jr.
December, 1981

I appreciate
your letting me
share the drama of
our megaton madness
with you.

This book
does not deal
with petty matters.

It tells how
to operate our lives—
and our world.

It tells us
how to stay alive!

The mess
we've brought upon ourselves
is a most perilous
and challenging one.

The broad picture
pieced together here
will show you
the immensity of
the nuclear dangers,
the futility of any defense
or protection,
the power of the new awareness
and your role
in the unfolding drama.

There is a phenomenon
I'd like to tell you about.

In it may lie
our only hope
of a future
for our species!

Here is the story
of the Hundredth Monkey:

The Japanese monkey,
Macaca fuscata,
has been observed in the wild
for a period of over 30 years.

In 1952,
on the island of Koshima
scientists were providing monkeys
with sweet potatoes
dropped in the sand.
The monkeys liked the taste
of the raw sweet potatoes,
but they found the dirt
unpleasant.

An 18-month-old female
named Imo
found she could solve the problem
by washing the potatoes
in a nearby stream.
She taught this trick
to her mother.
Her playmates also
learned this new way
and they taught their mothers, too.

This cultural innovation
was gradually picked up
by various monkeys
before the eyes of the scientists.

Between 1952 and 1958,
all the young monkeys
learned to wash
the sandy sweet potatoes
to make them more palatable.

Only the adults
who imitated their children
learned this social improvement.
Other adults
kept eating
the dirty sweet potatoes.

Then something startling took place.
In the autumn of 1958,
a certain number of Koshima monkeys
were washing sweet potatoes—
the exact number is not known.

Let us suppose
that when the sun rose one morning
there were 99 monkeys
on Koshima Island
who had learned
to wash their sweet potatoes.

Let's further suppose
that later that morning,
the hundredth monkey
learned to wash potatoes.

THEN IT HAPPENED!

By that evening
almost everyone in the tribe
was washing sweet potatoes
before eating them.

The added energy
of this hundredth monkey
somehow created
an ideological breakthrough!

But notice.
The most surprising thing
observed by these scientists
was that the habit
of washing sweet potatoes
then spontaneously jumped
over the sea—

Colonies of monkeys
on other islands
and the mainland troop of monkeys
at Takasakiyama
began washing
their sweet potatoes!*

*_Lifetide_ by Lyall Watson, pp. 147-148. Bantam Books, 1980. This book gives other fascinating details.

Thus, when a certain critical number
achieves an awareness,
this new awareness
may be communicated
from mind to mind.

Although the exact number may vary,
the Hundredth Monkey Phenomenon
means that when only
a limited number of people
know of a new way,
it may remain
the consciousness property
of these people.

But there is a point at which
if only one more person
tunes-in to a new awareness,
a field is strengthened
so that this awareness
reaches almost everyone!

The experiments of Dr. J. B. Rhine
at Duke University
repeatedly demonstrated
that individuals
can communicate private information
to each other
even though located
in different places.

We now know
that the strength
of this extrasensory communication
can be amplified
to a powerfully effective level
when the consciousness
of the "hundredth person"
is added.

Your awareness
is needed
in saving the world
from nuclear war.

You may be
the "Hundredth Monkey" . . . .

You may furnish
the added consciousness energy
to create
the shared awareness
of the urgent necessity
to rapidly achieve
a nuclear-free world.

"If I knew then
what I know now,
I never would have helped
to develop the bomb,"
spoke George Kistiakowsky,
an advisor to President Eisenhower
who worked on the
Manhattan Project.

Let's look at
the almost incredible
nuclear monster
we have created
in the last
forty years
on planet Earth . . . .

Herbert Scoville, Jr., former deputy director for research of the Central Intelligence Agency warns,

The unfortunate situation is that today we are moving—sliding downhill—toward the probability or the likelihood that a nuclear conflict will actually break out—and that somebody will use one of these nuclear weapons in a conflict or perhaps even by accident.

NUCLEAR WAR IS BAD FOR YOUR LIFE

The only result
of a substantial
nuclear exchange
would be a hollow victory
in which the "winners"
would be no better off
than the losers.

An all-out nuclear war
could make our planet
uninhabitable
for a million years!

A nuclear war
can end
the way we live.

It cannot be won—
it can only be lost.

Winning equals losing.

The word "war"
is too mild
to apply to
this nuclear craziness.

Suppose you and your family
are rafting down
an unexplored river.

Most of your attention
is on steering the raft
away from the rocks
and keeping it
off the banks
so that it will not
get damaged or stranded.

Several miles downstream
unknown to you
lies a huge waterfall
that will fling you
and your family
on the rocks below.

It is easy to miss
the significance
of certain signals
that are coming to you.

You have noticed a distant,
rumbling background sound.
But what does it mean?
You can see a mist
in the air ahead of you.
There's nothing alarming
that seems to call for
your immediate attention.

And, besides,
you are so busy
guiding the raft
and keeping it off the rocks
that you don't want to think
of anything else
right now.

Maybe the rumbling
will go away . . . .

But the distant rumbling
is getting louder.

We can ignore it—
or we can use
our intelligent minds
to inform us
of the dangers
we must avoid.

What are the signs
and the scientific data
that are so easy for us
to ignore—
but which are giving us
a clear warning
of a certain catastrophe
that lies ahead
if we remain
on our present course? *

*In 1954, actors John Wayne, Susan Hayward, Agnes
Moorehead and producer Dick Powell filmed "The
Conquerer" on the sandy dunes outside St. George, Utah.
We had previously conducted a number of atomic bomb
tests in Nevada about 150 miles away. For three months,
the filmmakers were breathing the dust laced with
radioactive plutonium fallout. Twenty-five years later
John Wayne, Susan Hayward, Agnes Moorehead and Dick
Powell had all died of cancer. Of the "220 people in the
cast and crew, ninety-one had contracted cancer by late
1980, and half of the cancer victims had died of the
disease." From *Killing Our Own* by Harvey Wasserman
and Norman Solomon, p. 81, Dell Publishing Company,
Inc., 1982.

In 1970, a pediatrician
in Grand Junction, Colorado,
noticed an increase
in cleft palate,
cleft lip
and other birth defects.

The homes of these people
had been built
with waste rock and sand
from a uranium refining operation!

The University of Colorado
Medical Center
obtained federal funds
to investigate this.

But these funds
were cut off
a year later.

Why?

Navajo Indians
who went down
into uranium mines
in Arizona
have died—
and are right now dying—
of lung cancer,
previously rare among Navajos.

In a recent study,
Dr. Gerald Buker pointed out
that the risk factor
of lung cancer
among Navajo uranium miners
increases by at least 85%!

R obert Minogue and Karl Goller
of the Nuclear Regulatory Commission
jointly wrote on September 11, 1978:

> The evidence mounts that, within the
> range of exposure levels encountered
> by radiation workers, there is no
> threshold, i.e., a level which can be
> assumed as safe in an absolute sense . . . .
> any amount of radiation has a finite
> probability of inducing a health effect,
> e.g., cancer.*

All exposure,
however small,
has a cumulative effect
on your body.

It all adds up
over your entire lifetime.

Shut Down, p. 72. The Book Publishing Co., 156 Drakes
  Lane, Summertown, TN 38483. 1979.
  In the nuclear honeymoon decades of the forties and
  fifties, the harmful effects of nuclear radiation on human
  health were underestimated by as much as ten thousand
  times! Ibid, p. 167.

Nuclear submarine workers
at Portsmouth, New Hampshire,
are developing cancer
at a rate that is double
the expected incidence.

Dr. Helen Caldicott,
author of *Nuclear Madness*,
was invited to speak
to a meeting of these workers,
but only four men appeared.

They told her
that the Navy
had threatened them
with the loss
of their jobs
if they came
to hear her talk.

Are jobs more important
than life itself?

In November, 1980,
a group of physicians and scientists
held a symposium
at the University of California
in Berkeley.
At this symposium
Dr. Kosta Tsipis,
Professor of Physics,
Massachusetts Institute of Technology,
stated,

NUCLEAR
WAR
IS BAD FOR
YOUR
EYES

> . . . our earth is surrounded by a thin
> layer of ozone. Ozone is a particular
> isotope of oxygen that has the lovely
> property of absorbing much of the
> ultraviolet rays of the sun. The ultra-
> violet rays of the sun are the ones that
> cause skin burns. When you go to the
> beach and you get sunburned, that's
> what does it. In addition, the ultra-
> violet rays of the sun blind eyes that
> are exposed to them for any period of
> time. The very fact that we can exist on
> this earth—that there is a fauna,
> animals with eyes on this earth—is
> based on the existence of the ozone
> layer that filters out most of the ultra-

violet rays of the sun and therefore allows us to survive.

What happens when a nuclear weapon explodes is that a very large number of nitrogen oxides are generated by the radiation that flies out from the explosion. As a matter of fact, a one-megaton weapon will generate 10^{32} molecules of nitrogen oxides. These molecules are lifted up together with the fireball, and reach (for a one-megaton weapon) the altitude of say 50, 60, 70 thousand feet, where the ozone is. At that point, these molecules will start eating up the ozone—literally—taking it away from circulation ... for long periods of time. It is a very complex photochemical process, but we know that it occurs .... The National Academy of Sciences felt quite sure to state that if you have exploded ... in a very short period of time 50% of the weapons that will be available in the arsenals of the Soviet Union and the United States by 1985, this simultaneous explosion will create enough nitrogen oxides to take out 50 to 70% of the ozone layer above the northern hemisphere and 30 to 40% of the ozone layer in the southern hemisphere, because we assume that all of these explosions will take place in the northern hemisphere ....

The latest word out of the scientific laboratories is that a 20% depletion of the ozone layer will allow enough ultra-violet light to come to earth that it will blind all unprotected eyes. Now, we can all wear glasses, but the animals and the birds will not wear glasses, and they will all be blinded and they will all eventually die. And this is the largest-scale ecological catastrophe that one can imagine—that all the fauna on the earth will be blinded and eventually die.

I can think of nothing else that is a more massive ecological dislocation—to use a mild word. The entire ecosystem will collapse. Because if we don't have insects, for example, to pollenate the flowers, we won't have fruit . . . . The whole thing collapses, and that is what will happen, most probably, if only 50% of the weapons in the arsenals of the two superpowers in 1985 were to be exploded within a few days in a nuclear war.*

NUCLEAR WAR IS BAD FOR ANIMALS

*A brilliant 48-minute videotape and 16 mm film of this important conference, entitled "The Last Epidemic: The Medical Consequences of Nuclear War," are available from the Resource Center for Nonviolence, Box 2324, Santa Cruz, CA 95063 or from Physicians for Social Responsibility, 23 Main St., Watertown, MA 02172. You may wish to buy a videotape or rent the film to share it in your community.

35

"Massive ecological dislocation"
will not be your problem
if you're near a bomb
when it goes off!

If you're within a few miles
of a nuclear detonation,
you'll be incinerated
on the spot!

And if you survive the blast,
what does the future promise?

The silent
but deadly radiation,
either directly
or from fallout,
in a dose of 400 rems
could kill you
within two weeks.

Your hair would fall out,
your skin would be covered
with large ulcers,
you would vomit
and experience diarrhea
and you would die
of infection
or massive bleeding
as your white blood cells
and platelets
stopped working.

If you have less exposure
to this deadly radioactivity,
you may develop leukemia
in five years.

**Hiroshima survivors
were thirty times more likely
to have this fatal disease
than the unexposed population!***

*Between 1945 and 1963 several hundred thousand soldiers
  were marched through areas where the Nevada atomic
  weapons tests were conducted. The rate of leukemia
  among these men had been 400 times the national
  average! *Shut Down*, p. 165.

  A battery operated geiger counter that will alert you to
nuclear radiation is available from Solar Electronics, 156
Drakes Lane, Summertown, TN 38483. Bear in mind that
a geiger counter only measures the radiation from external
sources such as nuclear power plant ventings, highway
spills, or industrial and military exposure. The greatest
danger comes from the radioactive cesium, strontium and
plutonium atoms that you eat or breathe. These agents of
death in your own body internally emit radiation that
constantly bombards the genes of the nearby cells. This
subtle (but perhaps more deadly radiation) from inside
your body is not measured by a geiger counter.

A smaller amount of exposure
sets you up for cancer
in twelve or more years.

Even a tiny invisible
particle of plutonium
is so radioactive
that it can cause cancer
or alter your genes
so that your children
may be deformed at birth!

Plutonium has been called
"thalidomide forever."

*Dr. John Gofman is the co-discoverer of uranium-233
and a leading medical researcher. In his 908-page book
Radiation and Human Health (Sierra Club Books,
San Francisco, 1981) he tells exactly how radiation produces
cancer, leukemia and birth defects. This book enables you
to estimate diminished life-expectancy from various radiation exposures. It evaluates the genetic consequences to
future generations of our current radiation exposures.
This comprehensive book can be ordered from the
Committee for Nuclear Responsibility, Box 11207,
San Francisco, CA 94101 for $29.95 postpaid.

Uranium,
mined from the earth,
is converted by
a processing facility
or a nuclear power plant
into plutonium,
strontium-90
and many other dangerous
radioactive poisons.

Plutonium is used
in making
high-yield nuclear bombs.
It has a half-life
of 24,400 years
and is poisonous
for at least
a half-million years.

NUCLEAR
WAR
IS BAD FOR
OVARIES

Dr. Helen Caldicott writes:

As a physician, I contend that nuclear technology threatens life on our planet with extinction. If present trends continue, the air we breathe, the food we eat, and the water we drink will soon be contaminated with enough radioactive pollutants to pose a potential health hazard far greater than any plague humanity has ever experienced. Unknowingly exposed to these radioactive poisons, some of us may be developing cancer right now. Others may be passing damaged genes, the basic chemical units which transmit hereditary characteristics, to future generations. And more of us will inevitably be affected unless we bring about a drastic reversal of our government's pronuclear policies.*

Nuclear Madness by Dr. Helen Caldicott, p. 1. Bantam Books, 1980. Copyright 1978, 1980 by Helen M. Caldicott. This book may be obtained from bookstores or from Vision Books, 790 Commercial Avenue, Coos Bay, Oregon 97420. Enclose $3.50, and we will pay the cost of packaging and shipping.

We are about to drown
in nuclear sewage.
We now have about
one hundred million gallons
of dangerous radioactive effluents
that no one knows what to do with.
And it's globally increasing
at a catastrophic rate.

There is no way to safely dispose
of this extremely dangerous,
corrosive, radioactive garbage
in leakproof containers
that will be continuously protected
by competent guards free from
war, earthquakes, floods and tornadoes
for hundreds of thousands of years!

What right have we
to burden future generations
with this ever-increasing threat
to their well-being?

We conducted
over 70 nuclear bomb tests
around the Marshall Islands
between 1946 and 1963.

Each mushroom cloud
scattered trillions
of plutonium atoms
throughout the world!*

Let's suppose
just one particle of plutonium
landed in a forest
near you.

It could rest on
a limb of a tree,
be stirred up in the air
and inhaled by a bird.

*By 1970 natives of the Marshall Islands were suffering
from increased incidence of cancer, retarded growth
and miscarriages.

This single plutonium particle
could create a radiation-induced
disease in the bird,
who would die prematurely.

Suppose the dead bird
decomposes in a field
and when driving by,
you breathe dust that contains
this invisible bit of plutonium.

This particle
of human-made plutonium
could ruin
the genetic regulating mechanism
in one of your cells
that prevents wild cancerous growths.

Your body could then
begin producing cancer cells . . . .

It's a matter
of probability and risk—
not certainty.

And this same deadly plutonium atom
could escape from your remains
and be recycled
with bad news consequences
for the next half-million years!

"All of us,
particularly the inhabitants
of the northern hemisphere,
carry some plutonium
in our lungs and other organs,"
according to Dr. John T. Edsell,
Professor of Biochemistry at Harvard.*

*Dr. John Gofman estimates that, because of the damage to
part of their clearance mechanism, the lungs of cigarette
smokers "might be a hundred times more sensitive to the
effects of plutonium."

The Savannah River nuclear plant, according to Dr. Carl Johnson of the Medical School of the University of Colorado, may have already polluted 1,000 square miles of Georgia and South Carolina with plutonium.*

*"And as late as 1979, radioiodine was measured in vegetation in nearby Columbia, Georgia, at a concentration that corresponds to a human thyroid dose of 24,000 millirems per year—320 times the amount permitted by the Environmental Protection Agency (EPA). High levels of tritium, which the plant releases routinely, have also been detected in the Savannah River and in local milk and vegetation . . . . Dr. Karl Z. Morgan, former director of the Health Physics Laboratory at Oak Ridge National Laboratories in Tennessee, notes that in 1969 the flesh of a deer taken from the plant site was discovered to have the equivalent of 2,250 millirems per year of cesium, or 90 times the EPA limit for a human." "Nuclear County" by Zachary Sklar, *Geo*, Vol. 3, p. 32, August 1981.

A 1975 study found that
more than 10,000 pounds
of this deadly chemical
are thinly dispersed
in the earth's atmosphere.

Your precious body
is probably already carrying
this hidden handmaiden
of genetic ruin
and death.*

Let's make sure
that we don't get
additional doses!★!#!

*Radioactive atoms are already in our food chain. The
United States Department of Agriculture in *Food, The
Yearbook of Agriculture 1959*, p. 118, reported that
strontium-90 from the United States and Russian atomic
bomb tests had scattered radioactive strontium-90 over
the entire earth. It was first detected in animal bones,
dairy products and soil in 1953. It is now in the bodies of
all human beings regardless of their age or where they live.
The *Bulletin of the Atomic Scientists*, Vol. XVII, No. 3,
p. 44, March 1962, stated that children growing up in the
United States have about 6 to 8 times more strontium-90
in their bones than their parents.

We've already
trapped ourselves
in a small degree
of irreversible
nuclear damage.

To avoid further harm
to ourselves
and our children,
the people
of the world
must somehow
avoid further
nuclear insanity.*

*A leakage on September 11, 1957, and again on May 11,
  1969, in the AEC Rocky Flats plutonium plant released
  plutonium near Denver, Colorado. There has been a 24%
  increase in cancer in men and a 10% increase in women
  in the portion of the Denver metropolitan area nearest
  to the Rocky Flats plutonium processing plant. For details
  write Jefferson County Health Department, 260 S. Kipling
  Street, Lakewood, CO 80226.

One million tons of TNT
is known as a megaton.
A grand total
of over three megatons
of nonnuclear explosives
were used in World War II
from 1941 to 1945.

Today, nuclear bombs
up to 20 megatons each
are poised for action.

Only one of these
could destroy a large city
and make the land dangerous
for eons!

Even larger nuclear warheads
are on the drawing boards!

Dr. Bernard Feld, professor, M.I.T., and the editor-in-chief of the *Bulletin of the Atomic Scientists* said,

Sometime later in this decade, military plans which are being seriously discussed now by the military establishments on both sides would lead to . . . an immediate exchange . . . in a nuclear war of something between 10,000 and 20,000 megatons each.

The fallout in the United States would be total. That is to say, there would be no areas, really, that could escape. There would be lethal fallout covering the entire United States and essentially the entire Soviet Union. Worldwide this would lead to something . . . somewhere in the region of, let's say, 20 radiation units per capita everywhere on earth.

And this I would regard as a situation which we would all have to consider to be absolutely intolerable.

And, therefore, it seems to me that we have no choice in the direction in which we have to move. The problem that faces us is not whether nuclear disarmament is feasible, but how we can go about convincing our leaders. And, presumably, they will be convinced when all the people, or at least a majority of the people, of our countries are convinced of the unacceptability of the current course of events in which missile is piled on top of missile, in which weapon is piled on top of weapon, and in which doctrines concerning their use are being proliferated not only in the insane superpowers but in other so-called civilized countries as well.

How are we going to convince ourselves that this is an intolerable direction, stop where we are, turn it around and eventually reduce these stockpiles . . . ?

David Hoffman points out,
"In a nuclear war,
the best defense
is not to have
an offense."*

War no longer functions
for settling disputes
between nations.

War itself
must be abolished
in the twentieth century—
just as slavery
was eliminated
during the nineteenth century.

Our survival demands
new ways
for operating
our civilization!

*David Hoffman is the co-founder of "Interhelp," Box
 4448, Arcata, CA 95521, a think tank focusing on
 practical ways to get us out of our nuclear predicament.

A single conventional bomb
can blow up the reactor rods
that fuel a power plant.

If Europe had nuclear power plants
during World War II,
our bombs could have
devastated the continent
and made it uninhabitable
for thousands of years
by radioactive pollution
of the air, food and water.*

NUCLEAR
WAR
IS BAD FOR
SURVIVAL

Any nuclear reactors anywhere
make us vulnerable
to aggression and fanaticism
by politicians and terrorists—
even if they don't have access
to nuclear bombs.

*A 1964 Atomic Energy Commission study showed that a
 serious nuclear accident could kill 45,000 people, injure
 100,000 and contaminate "an area the size of Pennsylvania."

When we even maintain
a supply of nuclear bombs
as a "deterrent,"
we are dangerously perpetuating
the illusion
that our safety and security
lie in nuclear materials.

Such a consciousness
makes inevitable
the competitive stockpiling
and future use
of these materials.

And the passions
of many military
and political leaders
and terrorists
are such that
sooner or later
they will unleash
every bit of destructiveness
they can get their hands on!

Have you ever felt
overconfident?

Have you ever felt
like taking a chance
just to see
how it comes out?

Have you ever felt so angry
that you were determined
to hurt someone
even if you hurt yourself, too?

Have you ever felt so depressed,
so discouraged,
that you
just didn't give a damn?

Have you ever felt
like kicking over a game
you couldn't win?*

*People close to Nixon in his last days in office reportedly
 deactivated the signal mechanism that our President can
 use to hurl our nuclear holocaust at Russia and
 destroy the world.

The United States and Russia
have enough military hardware
to destroy
every city on earth
seven times!

And other nations are scrambling
to acquire this dreadful
suicidal power!*

Why do we have to live
under these
perilous conditions?

*The U.S., Russia, France, Great Britain, Italy and West
 Germany are selling nuclear and conventional arms to
 other countries at the rate of over $350 million per day!
 It's sad to note that our economies and our diplomacy are
 developing a dependency on our roles as merchants
 of death.

Eventually,
every large or small country
on this planet could have a supply
of deadly nuclear bombs.

Nuclear bombs
are not that difficult to make . . . .

Eight thousand pounds
of plutonium and uranium
are now missing
from U.S. facilities,
according to the
Nuclear Regulatory Commission!

The insane arms race
is almost out of control.

Nuclear war by design
or by accident
is possible
and imminent!

IT COULD HAPPEN ANY MINUTE!

"**N**uclear war,"
according to Roger Fisher,
Professor of Law at Harvard,
"is not a solution.
It is worse
than any problem
it might 'solve.'"

An all-out
nuclear war
between the U.S. and Russia
could kill
hundreds of millions of people
and subject the survivors
to radiation sicknesses—
and cause countless mutations
of the genetic blueprints
of our species.*

*If our nuclear insanity continues, our great-grandchildren
  may be so mutated that they cannot even be classified
  as members of our species, *Homo sapiens.*

"Nuclear weapons
aren't weapons—
they're an obscenity,"
said Dr. Marvin Goldberger, President,
California Institute of Technology.

According to Dr. Herbert L. Abrams
of the Harvard Medical School,
the corpses produced
by a nuclear war
between Russia and the United States
if laid end to end
would reach from
the earth to the moon.

Could any worthwhile human desire
however right, good or needed
be actually achieved
by this sacrifice
of the human race?

Rear Admiral Gene R. LaRocque, United States Navy (retired), suggests that a nuclear war may be started by mechanical mishaps and electronic and personnel errors:

> . . . one of our strategic submarines, the *George Washington*, ran right into a Japanese ship just a few months ago and sank it! That's one of our best missile submarines! . . . We've lost two of our nuclear attack submarines that sank in the ocean and we don't know why to this day—the *Scorpion* and the *Thresher*. And earlier this year one of our missiles was accidentally fired from Arkansas because a mechanic dropped a wrench . . . .

> We've had several incidents where nuclear weapons have literally fallen out of airplanes, literally just fallen through the bomb bays. Probably the most interesting one is the one that fell out of a strategic bomber in the Carolinas some years ago . . . . landed in Carolina in a swamp, and they looked all over for that nuclear weapon. We haven't found it yet . . . .*

*The Defense Department bought the land, put a fence around it, and now it's a nuclear safety area! From a talk given on October 31, 1981 at a Los Angeles symposium organized by Physicians for Social Responsibility and the Council for a Livable World.

Daniel Ellsberg,
who was an assistant to former
Secretary of Defense McNamara,
reminds us of an accident in 1961
when an Air Force plane
carrying a 24-megaton bomb
crashed in North Carolina.

On crash impact five of the six
interlocking safety mechanisms
on the bomb failed!
Only one switch kept the bomb
from unleashing the equivalent of
1,000 Nagasaki-type explosions!*

We've been lucky
so far!

*From *Survival* newsletter, Sept.-Nov. 1981, published by
Alliance for Survival, 1720 N. La Brea Avenue, Los
Angeles, CA 90046. You can receive their magazine and
support their nonprofit work by your $15 membership.
They are working toward zero nuclear weapons, stopping
the arms race, banning nuclear power and meeting
human needs.

A Russian airplane
carrying a nuclear weapon
crashed in
the Sea of Japan.

U.S. submarines
carrying nuclear missiles
have collided
with Russian ships.

By mistake,
we dropped on Spain
four plutonium bombs
which fortunately
did not explode.

Oops—so sorry!

The failure of a 46¢ computer part
has produced a false signal
that Russian missiles
were on the way.

NUCLEAR WAR IS BAD FOR INTERNATIONAL RELATIONS

On November 9, 1979,
a reportedly fail-safe computer
responded to a war games tape
by turning on
all American early warning systems
around the world!

On June 3 and again on June 6, 1980,
computer errors in our warning system
began a rapid chain of events
that could have ruined the planet.

You and I may have been
only minutes from nuclear death
when these technical errors
were spotted!!!*

*Military folks will protest that, while true, the above are
unfair statements. They haven't blown us apart yet, have
they?

What if an error is not detected within minutes?

U_p until
the last half
of this century,
civil defense was
usually protective
against ordinary bombs.

With less than
thirty minutes warning
of a missile attack,
we can forget it!

The fire storm of a nuclear missile
will turn most underground shelters
into crematoriums, anyway.

**TODAY PROTECTIVE MEASURES
ARE INEFFECTIVE,
AND ULTIMATELY
FUTILE.**

Nuclear bombs
are so hopelessly devastating
that at the November, 1980
Conference of the
Physicians for Social Responsibility,
Dr. H. Jack Geiger said,

> It is my belief that any physician who
> even takes part in so-called emergency
> medical disaster planning—specifically
> to meet the problem of nuclear attack—
> is committing a profoundly unethical
> act. He is deluding himself or herself,
> colleagues, and by implication the pub-
> lic at large, into the false belief that
> mechanisms of survival in any mean-
> ingful social sense are possible.*

*For more information write Physicians for Social Respon-
sibility, P.O. Box 144, Watertown, MA 02172.

Albert Einstein warned:
"We must never
relax our efforts
to arouse
in the people of the world,
and especially in their governments,
an awareness
of the unprecedented disaster
which they are absolutely certain
to bring on themselves
unless there is
a fundamental change
in their attitudes
toward one another
as well as in their concept
of the future.

"The unleashed power
of the atom
has changed everything
except our way of thinking."

NUCLEAR
WAR
IS BAD FOR
CIVIL
DEFENSE

Nothing is worth
playing Russian roulette
with the journey
of *Homo sapiens.*

As you and I
live out our lives
and set up the way
for future generations,
let us resolve
to avoid
nuclear destruction.

Why let ourselves
be wiped out
by not responding
to the clear signs
of future catastrophe?*

*See *The Fate of the Earth* by Jonathan Schell. Alfred A.
Knopf, Inc., 1982. It places the issue in a large perspective
with a brilliant analysis of the forces at play. *The Fate of
the Earth* is an important guide at this crucial time.

C arl Sagan,
**professor of astronomy
at Cornell University
and creator
of the "Cosmos" series,
said:**

What a waste it would be after 4 billion
tortuous years of evolution if the
dominant organism contrived its own
self-destruction. We are the first species
to have devised the means. There is no
issue more important than the
avoidance of nuclear war. It is
incredible for any thinking person not
to be concerned with this issue. No
species is guaranteed tenured life on
this planet. We are privileged to be
alive and to think. We have the
privilege to affect the future.

Since nuclear missiles
fly both ways,
neither the United States nor Russia
can make itself more secure
by making the other
less secure.

Nuclear weapons
can no longer provide us
with security.

Our choice is clear:

A non-nuclear future or none at all!!!

Our life on the planet
is more important
than money
or military power!

Do we have to be
such fanatics
that we destroy the world
by squabbling
over conflicting ideas?

Is a "cerebral itch"
more important
than life itself?

Is human destiny
a hectic trip
from Adam to Atom?

All around us
we're getting messages
loud and clear:

The danger of the annihilation of human civilization should not be made the subject of theoretical arguments, but be used as a basis for creating a common awareness of the alarming situation the world is facing today and of the need for exercising the political will to search for acceptable solutions.

*Report of the Secretary-General of the United Nations.**

And again:

The overwhelming priority to do away with nuclear arms has not penetrated the collective consciousness or conscience of the general public . . . . Nuclear arms must not just be limited, they must be eliminated.

*Rev. Maurice McCrackin
Community Church of Cincinnati*

*"General and Complete Disarmament, Comprehensive Study on Nuclear Weapons," (A/35/392, page 151, September 12, 1980.)

Rear Admiral LaRocque

warns us:

> It's very important for all of us today to
> realize that the Soviet Union is not
> the enemy. Nuclear war is the enemy.
> We're going to have to learn to live
> with the Russians or we and the
> Russians are going to die at about the
> same time.

So urgent is the situation

that we must shortcut

through our usual ways of thinking.

Humanity and world peace must be given priority above everything else.

NUCLEAR WAR IS BAD FOR PLANET EARTH

*Rear Admiral LaRocque is now the Director of the Center
For Defense Information, 303 Capital Gallery West,
600 Maryland Ave., S.W., Washington, D.C. 20024.

As individuals
we must act affirmatively
and stop supporting
the drift toward
nuclear holocaust.

Dale Bridenbaugh, Richard Hubbard
and Gregory Minor
took their stand
and resigned
from highly paying positions
as nuclear engineers
at General Electric
on February 2, 1976.

They told the Joint Committee on Atomic Energy:

When we first joined the General Electric Nuclear Energy Division, we were very excited about the idea of this new technology—atomic power—and the promise of a virtually limitless source of safe, clean and economic energy for this and future generations. But now . . . the promise is still unfulfilled. The nuclear industry has developed to become an industry of narrow specialists, each promoting and refining a fragment of the technology, with little comprehension of the total impact on our world system . . . . We [resigned] because we could no longer justify devoting our life energies to the continued development and expansion of nuclear fission power—a system we believe to be so dangerous that it now threatens the very existence of life on this planet.

The problem
of nuclear poisoning
of the planet
can only be solved
by educating
the people on earth
about the nuclear
facts of life.

The people of Russia,
the United States
and all other countries
can be made aware
of the nuclear peril—

When the people of this earth
know the facts,
they will not want to live
poised on the brink
of nuclear annihilation!

"The war planning process of the past has become totally obsolete. ATTACK IS NOW SUICIDE," said Thomas J. Watson, Jr., former Ambassador to the Soviet Union and President of IBM.

Watson warns us against:

> "... the illusion that we cannot sign treaties with the Russians because they systematically violate them.
>
> Let us be clear about this: there are major differences between our two countries. Soviet values are diametrically opposed to ours. Contention between us on a global scale is a fact of life. Suspicion is the keynote of our relations.
>
> But having said that, let me add this: on the evidence, the Soviets do keep agreements provided each side has an interest in the other's keeping the agreement, and provided each side can verify compliance for itself.*

*Keynote address at Harvard's 330th commencement on June 4, 1981.

In 1958
a Russian nuclear installation
exploded at Kyshtym.
Radioactive clouds
devastated the countryside
for hundreds of miles.
This area of the Ural Mountains
is now a wasteland
that cannot be inhabited
for millennia.

It's interesting to note
the U.S. Government
hid this CIA report
for almost 20 years.

It only came to light
in 1977 under the
Freedom of Information Act.

In 1981 George Kennan,
former Ambassador to Moscow,
and one of our foremost
authorities on Russia,
called for immediate, across-the-board
50% reductions
in all kinds of nuclear arms
as a first step by both sides.
He pointed out:

NUCLEAR WAR IS BAD FOR RUSSIA

> We have gone on piling weapon upon
> weapon, missile upon missile, new
> levels of destructiveness upon old ones,
> helplessly, almost involuntarily, like
> victims of some sort of hypnotism, like
> men in a dream, like lemmings heading
> for the sea.

> And the result is that today we have
> achieved—we and the Russians
> together—in the creation of these
> devices and their means of delivery,
> levels of redundancy of such grotesque
> dimensions as to defy rational under-
> standing. What a confession of intel-
> lectual poverty it would be, what a
> bankruptcy of intelligent statesman-
> ship, if we had to admit that such
> blind, senseless acts of destruction were
> the best we could do!

Dr. Jim Muller
of the Harvard Medical School
reports that:

In March, 1981 at a conference held by the International Physicians for the Prevention of Nuclear War, Dr. Yevgeni I. Chazov, Deputy Minister of Health of the U.S.S.R. and cardiologist to Chairman Brezhnev and other Kremlin leaders, revealed that he had spent 35 minutes on national Soviet television discussing the medical consequences of nuclear war. The conference itself was covered in detail by *Pravda,* with a circulation of over 10 million, *Izvestia,* over 8 million, and so on. Statements about the impossibility of surviving nuclear war and appeals to world leaders to prevent it were printed intact.*

---

*In June, 1982, Dr. Muller, with Dr. Bernard Lown and Dr. John Pastore, appeared on Soviet television with Dr. Chazov and two other Russian physicians. Dr. Chazov said,"We have come here openly and honestly to tell the people about our movement, whose main objective is the preservation of life on earth." They discussed such topics as the effects of a one-megaton bomb on a city, medical care for the victims and the long-term effects of radiation fallout. The one-hour telecast was seen by an estimated 100 million Russians and it was not censored.

Dwight D. Eisenhower,
who served as a five-star general
in World War II
and who also served
as President of the United States,
could speak as
"... one who has witnessed
the horror and the
lingering sadness of war—
as one who knows that
another war
could utterly destroy
this civilization
which has been
so slowly
and painfully built
over thousands of years ...."

NUCLEAR
WAR
IS BAD FOR
TAXPAYERS

In 1953, Eisenhower said,
"Every gun that is made,
every warship launched,
every rocket fired,
signifies in a final sense
a theft from those
who hunger and are not fed—
those who are cold and not clothed.

"This world in arms
is not spending money alone—
it is spending
the sweat of its laborers,
the genius of its scientists,
the houses of its children."

By 1959,
this general
and statesman said,

"I like to believe
that people in the long run
are going to do more
to promote peace
than are governments.

"INDEED, I THINK THAT PEOPLE
WANT PEACE SO MUCH
THAT ONE OF THESE DAYS
GOVERNMENTS HAD BETTER
GET OUT OF THEIR WAY
AND LET THEM HAVE IT."

The Council for a Livable World
has pointed out
that military expenditures
of themselves are destructive
to human life—
even if the weapons
they stockpile
are never used.*

*The Council for a Livable World was founded in 1962 by
the eminent nuclear physicist Dr. Leo Szilard to combat
the menace of nuclear war and strengthen national security
through rational arms control. The Council continues to
pursue its objectives by blending the resources of its
knowledgeable scientists with the skills of practical
politics, and by concentrating its efforts on the U.S. Senate
which has unique advise and consent powers in foreign
affairs. You may help by sending a contribution to Council
for a Livable World, 11 Beacon Street, Boston, MA 02108.

The people of Earth
are now spending
one million dollars per minute
on armaments!

Once we stop preparing
to blast each other apart,
we will find
that we can easily solve
all the world's hunger,
water and shelter problems.*

*More than $18 billion in arms sales were made to Third
World countries in 1980—up from $8 billion in 1975.
  Let them eat—guns?!?

What can
you and I do
about the biggest problem
our world
has ever faced?

In case you are feeling
that there is nothing
you can do
about the increasing
nuclear menace
that hangs
over our heads,
remember the story
of the Hundredth Monkey.

You may be
the Hundredth Monkey!

Your own awareness
and action
can be the added energy
needed to make the difference
between life or death
for you,
your family—
and all of us.

Dr. Caldicott reminds us,

> The power of an aroused public is unbeatable. Vietnam and Watergate proved that. It must be demonstrated again. It is not yet too late, for while there is life there is hope. There is no cause for pessimism, for already I have seen great obstacles surmounted. Nor need we be afraid, for I have seen democracy work.*

*Nuclear Madness by Dr. Helen Caldicott, p. 93. Bantam Books, 1980. Copyright 1978, 1980 by Helen M. Caldicott.

Mass action is effective.

Eighty thousand people
in June, 1977
marched in Australia
demanding that uranium
be left in the ground
where it belongs.

This protest was successful!

In Germany,
after experiencing nuclear protests,
West German Chancellor
Helmut Schmidt said,
"One cannot simply force
nuclear energy
down people's throats."

An initiative is now under way
in the State of California
to place on the ballot
The California Bilateral Nuclear
Weapons Freeze Initiative:

"The People of the State of California,
recognizing that the safety and security
of the United States must be paramount
in the concerns of the American people;
and further recognizing that our
national security is reduced, not increased, by the growing danger of
nuclear war between the United States
and the Soviet Union which would
result in millions of deaths of people
in California and throughout the
nation; do hereby urge that the Government of the United States propose to
the Government of the Soviet Union
that both countries agree to immediate-
ly halt the testing, production and
further deployment of all nuclear
weapons, missiles and delivery systems
in a way that can be checked and veri-
fied by both sides.*

*Endorsed by the New York State Assembly, Oregon State
Legislature, Massachusetts State Legislature, National Council
of Churches, American Friends Service Committee, Catholic
Archdiocese of San Francisco, National Conference of Black
Mayors, Interfaith Center to Reverse the Arms Race,
Unitarian-Universalist Association, and many other groups.

The United Nations organization
with its worldwide offices
will help if requested:

> Once there is an initiative from a
> region, the countries and regional
> organizations concerned should be
> able, upon their request and in the
> manner they wish, to draw to the
> fullest extent on the resources and
> possibilities of the United Nations
> system.*

Many groups and organizations
today stand ready to help us.

You can probably find meetings
for disarmament or world peace
that are happening
only minutes from your home.

They need your energy
to do the job for all of us.

*Report of the Secretary-General of the United Nations,
"General and Complete Disarmament, Study on All the
Aspects of Regional Disarmament." (Page 64, A/35/416,
October 8, 1980)

Here's some good news.

In June, 1981
a Gallup poll
asked Americans,
"Do you think
that the United States
should or should not
meet with the Soviet Union this year
to try to reach agreement
on nuclear disarmament?"

Eighty percent said
we should meet,
thirteen percent said
we should not,
with seven percent
undecided. *

*Nuclear War: What's in It For You? by Ground Zero is an
excellent book that will increase your nuclear awareness.
It is available from Pocket Books for $2.95.

If you wish to use this book
to do your part
in awakening people,
we can help you.

We will send you
an unbroken case
of 40 books for $40
payable in advance.
(We will pay shipping
anywhere in the United States.)

To really do it,
let's work together
in this way:

> If you order unbroken
> cases of 100 books, we
> will send them for only
> 60¢ each postpaid!!! Be
> sure to send payment in
> advance.*

*All orders should be sent to Vision Books, 790 Commercial Avenue, Coos Bay, Oregon 97420. Cartons containing 40 books will be shipped throughout the world for $50 for surface mail or $90 for airmail.

In addition to mass action,
we must alter
the separating mental habits
that created
the nuclear problem
from the start.

Let's examine
the change in consciousness
that must take place
for four billion of us
to get along together
on planet Earth.

How we think and feel
has got us into
this nuclear problem.

The way to our survival
lies in altering
how we think and feel.

We must use the power
of our collective consciousness
as we learn
to focus on peace—
and human togetherness.

The men and women
of the nuclear nations
must be willing
to give up their
PLUTONIUM
SECURITY
BLANKETS.

Instead we must
REALLY be willing
to REALLY listen
so we can
REALLY understand
what's REALLY bothering them.

We must get behind
emotional rigidity,
intellectual jargon and
logic-tight compartments
of the mind.

We must realize
that there are
no simple right answers.

We must stop risking
the survival of our planet
by demanding that we
always get our way.
If we always get our way,
there is no real negotiation.

Together we must develop
effective understandings
based on both sides
working together to create
mutually acceptable solutions
that we can all live with.

It's our
separate-self mental habits
that are the cause
of our survival predicament.

The bomb is not
the real problem—
it's only an effect
of our attitudes.

Our mental habits
of understanding events
in an "us-vs.-them" perception
rather than
an "us-and-them" insight
are creating
a devastating mental,
emotional
and moral separateness
in our minds.

If the human race
can't learn
to get along with itself,
it will soon
exterminate itself.

A group of our top scientists
working in the Manhattan Project
during World War II
developed the atomic bomb
from textbook theory to Hiroshima
in only four years!

What would happen
if an equally dedicated group
backed by our nation's resources
worked together to create
a world consciousness
of our common humanity
and a unity
of our human hearts and minds
that would make
all armaments useless?

Any problem
created by the human mind
can be solved by the human mind.

What's stopping us?

If you had
a highly contagious,
often fatal, disease,
you would care enough
about other people
to try to avoid
transmitting it.

Could the
expectations and demands
that make you feel hatred,
alienation
and a "me-vs.-them" separateness
be considered
a disease?

NUCLEAR
WAR
IS BAD FOR
WAR
VETERANS

Such emotion-backed demands
are more deadly
to the survival
of the human race
than all contagious diseases
added together!!!

Remember this the next time
your mind makes you experience
hatred and hard-heartedness.

If we want humankind
to survive into the next century,
we can no longer afford
to transmit the deadly viruses
of hatred, noncaring
and forcefully getting one's way
that lead to murder, assassination
and ultimately
to nuclear destruction.

Increasingly our minds
have put great energy into
three forms of separateness
that make us create
thoughts and actions
that result in
a lethal threat
to our continued life
on planet Earth!*

*See *No Boundary* by Ken Wilber. Center Publications,
1979. This is a discussion of how our minds create
division and separateness.

First,
your mind
is divided
against itself.

You have become
self-conscious,
self-downing,
self-critical,
and in too many ways
have lost
your deeper levels
of appreciating yourself.

Have you sometimes noticed
that when you're feeling
most separate
from someone else,
behind it all
your mind is just
not feeling good
about you?

Secondly, your mind
has become divided
against your own body.

Your thinking has obstructed
the free flow
of your feelings.
Your mental activity
constantly crowds out
your experiencing
the aliveness
of your body.

You have neglected your body
and instead put your energy
into activities involving
pride, prestige
and that ever-seductive "success"
that have not
brought you happiness
or peace of mind.

Thirdly,
just as your mind
has become
divided against itself
and against the body
which houses it,
it has also increasingly
alienated itself
from your four billion cousins
that are here and now
sharing the planet
with you.

In too many situations
we automatically
experience people
as "them"—not "us."

These jungle-type
habits of mind
are dangerous
to our species.

In the millions of years
in which our ancestors
were surviving
in the jungles,
it was important
for their minds
to create an instant
"self-vs.-other" perception.

For animals
eat other animals
and no species can survive
if all of its members
are eaten up.

This instant perception
of "otherness"
is basic to survival
for animals in the jungle.

We can learn
a more effective way
to make our lives work.

We are still creating
a "jungle"
of our civilized lives
by continuing the operation
of our "us-vs.-them"
mental habits.

We're all
in this together!

"Love alone,"
wrote Teilhard de Chardin,
"is capable of uniting living beings
in such a way
as to complete and fulfill them,
for it alone
takes them and joins them
by what is deepest
in themselves."

UNDERSTANDING,
COOPERATION
AND
LOVE
ARE
THE
KEYS
TO
HUMAN
SURVIVAL!

The problem I find
in trying to go
from the separate-self
to the consciousness
of my unified-self
is that my ego operates
under the illusory programming
that in order
to like or love you,
I must like or love
everything
you do or say.

NUCLEAR WAR IS BAD FOR SMILES

I identify you
with your thoughts
or your actions.

I lose sight of the fact
that your thoughts and actions
just reflect
your life experiences
and your training.

111

I may crystallize my mind
against what you do or say
and fail to notice
your good intentions . . .
which usually are
just like mine!

Even if you drop
a bomb on me
your purpose
is to settle arguments—
and create peace!

These are
good intentions—
just like mine!

You just need
a more effective way
to realize
your positive intentions!

A stereo set
is not the record it plays.

If a record is scratchy,
we don't throw out
the stereo set.
All we have to do
is change the record.

NUCLEAR
WAR
IS BAD FOR
MONKEYS

We don't have to
reject a human being
because we don't like
his or her programming.

We can just make it clear
that we like the person—
but we don't like
a particular action.

And our thoughts and actions
can change
because they're not us—
in our essence.

I have the direct experience
that in my essence
I am something apart
from the mental habits
that spin out my personality
and the current soap opera
of my life.

Thus I can dislike
a person's behavior
and still feel that
this is a human being
who like me
is just trying
to make life work
using the programming
we picked up
when we were young.

Your thoughts and actions
are only a set
of mental habits
in a state of flux
as you evolve
from stage to stage
of your life's growth.

All of us
have done mean,
sloppy and uncaring things
that we wish
we hadn't done.

I always hope
that you
won't identify me
with the things
that I've done
that were unskillful responses
to life situations.

The mind can be trained
to nurture
a "me-_and_-you" consciousness
in which
patience and understanding
will compassionately harmonize
the flow of our activities
so that we all want
to help each other
work things out.

We can
develop an awareness
that things aren't
problem-free for me
until they're
problem-free for you!

This applies equally
to relationships
between individuals
or between countries.

When I create
my experience of you
I may forget
that you are not
your thoughts or actions.

I don't know you from inside—
as I experience myself.

I may forget
that in every important way
you are like me.

You have a human heart
that feels
pain and warmth,
sadness and happiness.

In your essence
and in your intentions
you are basically good—
just like me!

And my ego
is often too ready
to treat as important
all the differences
that my mind notices:
lifestyle, skin color,
social status,
educational background,
our differing ideas
and opinions
and on and on.

When I continually magnify
these outward signs,
I create the experience
that you are really
different from me.

It's time
we begin to realize
that you and I
are far more alike
than we are different.

We are all
fellow beings
travelling the road of life
together.

We don't live
in isolation.

We are all
interconnected.

We all live
in one world.

NUCLEAR
WAR
IS BAD FOR
UNITY

We are affected by
a lack of harmony
of any type
anywhere on the planet—
even if we're not
consciously aware of it.

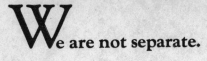We are not separate.

What we say and do
can affect the well-being
of all of us.

We know that
our health may be affected
if we live among
diseased people.

What we are beginning to learn
is that our peace of mind
may be affected
if we live among
disturbed people.

Our happiness may be affected
if we live among
unhappy people.

Our love may be affected
if we live among clashing,
unloving people.

122

And even the future
of our species
is affected
if various nations
are stockpiling
nuclear devices
designed
to destroy
each other.

The nuclear nations today
have created a total
of 50,000 nuclear devices—
each of which
is an expression
of the consciousness
of the separate-self.

These dangerous toys
enable some children of Earth,
pompously playing the roles
of military and political leaders,
to kill fellow humans
in other nations.

We pay a horrendous price
for this separate-self—
this "me-vs.-you"
jungle-type consciousness.

No matter what illusions
may dominate our minds,
nuclear devices
are suicidal
for our species.

Any perception
that our lives
are an "us-vs.-them" matter
is an illusion
and can only create
alienation, unhappiness—
and perhaps death.

If our species
is to survive,
it must replace
the illusions of separateness
with the emotional experiences
of acceptance, cooperation
and togetherness.

Instead of
"you <u>vs.</u> me"
it must become
"you <u>and</u> me"—
on this planet
together.

However much
our ideas and ideologies
may clash,
we must remember
that nothing is more important
for survival
and for happiness in life
than feelings of understanding
and commonness of human purpose.

All of the nations on earth
are acting like spoiled children
who are fighting over marbles.

Children forget
that their happiness comes
not from possession of the marbles,
but from the fun of playing together—
and from creating
the great adventure of life
together.

We can learn
to keep our squabbles
within bounds.

We can learn to disagree
without throwing each other
out of our hearts—
and thus create
rocklike hatreds.

We can become skillful
at changing
the desire systems
in our minds.

Whatever we
expect to get
by creating
hatred and separateness
even if "justified"
is always purchased
at far too great
a price.

Human love—
our heart-to-heart love—
is more valuable
than anything else.

If we have this,
we have enough.

Without this love
in our hearts,
nothing else
will be enough!

Kierkegaard said,
". . . to love human beings
is still the only thing
worth living for—
without that love,
you really do not live."

Let's not ruin our future
because of anything
that happened in the past.

Let us challenge
our present approaches
and rethink old assumptions.

Would you want
your children
to die
because your mind
is not flexible enough
to forgive?*

NUCLEAR WAR IS BAD FOR LOVE

*Bernard Benson in *The Peace Book* (Bantam Books, 1982) gives a sensitive new angle by letting a child ask the pertinent questions and give practical solutions. Philip Noel Baker (Co-chairman of the World Disarmament Campaign and winner of the Nobel Peace Prize) said, "Everyone who wants to live should read this book." It has been translated to Russian and the author was interviewed by children on TV in Moscow.

From the point of view
of our complex desire systems,
life will always
seem "imperfect."

WE WIN SOME
AND WE LOSE SOME.

Can we expand our hearts
so that we do not hate
even the proponents
of nuclear power?

Can we learn
to feel love and compassion
for the people involved
in perpetuating nuclear technology
even when they're
unable or unwilling
to understand the reasons
for our concern?

Always remember
that feelings of anger
and hatred and separateness
are our only problem.

Let's not try
to save the world
by increasing the problem!

The next step
in our growth
as individuals
and as a species
requires that our minds
experience the planetary urgency
of letting go
of separating mental habits
and demands
that close our hearts
to other people.

We are challenged
by our destiny
to increase our ability
to create with many people
the enjoyable experiences
of acceptance
and cooperation.

Individual and species survival
means increasing our tolerance,
our patience
and our understanding
so that we do not continue
to drive ourselves crazy
when people or situations
are not the way
we want them to be.

We can no longer afford
to create separateness
and alienation
if we want to get the most
from our lives.

We can still
want what we want.
We can think
it's only fair or right
to get it.

We can still put
gentle energy
into trying to change things.

But we must learn
not to throw people
out of our hearts.

We tear each other apart
too easily . . . .

We're all like kids,
taking our disagreements
and our differences
too seriously!

When will we learn
that it is only
our emotion-backed demands
that make us create
the internal experience
of unhappiness?

Our egos
and rational minds
are so good
at making us
feel and think
that the problem
of human separateness
lies in the outside world—
and not inside ourselves!

With practice,
this mental skill
of inner flexibility
will make us
even more effective
and powerful.

It takes a strong person
to be able
to lovingly
but directly communicate
what he or she wants
to someone
who disagrees—
and acts hostile.

You will increase your skill
in helping the world
when you learn
to be mentally flexible.

This means
being able to
constantly blend back
into creating an experience
of life as a whole
with appreciation,
cooperativeness
and love
for the people around you—
even when they oppose you.

We haven't yet
become effective
at operating our minds
and our emotions
to create that subtle blend
of both head and heart
that lets us use
our treasure chest
of inner wisdom.

This wisdom is kept
tightly locked up
when our egos and minds
run off the tapes
that continually create
the illusion of separateness.

Only by opening
our minds and hearts
will we find the rich,
intuitive wisdom
that always lies
within every human being—
even if it isn't used.

The conflicting energies
in our world
are so great today
that perhaps we need
the "millionth monkey"
to project the energy
of wholeness and cooperation—
of friendship and love,
of sharing life
on this planet
together.

Whatever That Critical Number Is, You Are Needed To Save Our Civilization.

NUCLEAR
WAR
IS BAD FOR
OUR
CIVILIZATION

You are essential!!!

It may be
that without you,
it will not happen
and our species
will hurtle itself
into partial
or complete destruction.

How do we play the game of saving the world?

To begin with,
you probably can't
help others understand
unless you have a grasp
of the scope
of the nuclear jeopardy
we all face.

NUCLEAR
WAR
IS BAD FOR
MENTAL
HEALTH

One of the most
readable and fascinating
books on this subject
is *Killing Our Own*
by Harvey Wasserman
and Norman Solomon.

This book tells about
the countless human deaths
already caused by
the Hiroshima and Nagasaki bombs,
the Nevada bomb tests,
the tests in the Pacific Islands,
uranium mining,
exposure in nuclear industries,
and the near meltdown
at the Three-Mile Island
nuclear power plant.

Killing Our Own may be obtained from bookstores
or from Dell Publishing Company, Inc., One Dag
Hammarskjold Plaza, New York, New York 10017
(Copyright, 1982).

Above all,
be creative—
and energetic.

Since the future
of both you and your family
is at stake,
turn on
the immense resources
of your mind.

Find the ways in which
you can flow your energy
into increasing
worldwide awareness
that the nuclear bomb mentality
must be eliminated.

The strength of our species
lies not in sharp fangs
or piercing claws.

It lies in our ability
to use our minds
to cooperate with each other
as we play
the games of life.

The same powerful minds
that created nuclear bombs
and intercontinental missiles
can also learn how
to create human unity
and cooperativeness.

We <u>can</u> save the world
from people-made disaster—
when we set the goal high
and add our determination
and our persistence.

Appoint yourself
as a roving Ambassador
of the State
of Loving and Caring.

Will you accept
your share of
the responsibility
for creating
the Hundredth Monkey energy
that will change
the consciousness
of the entire planet?

We can tilt the scales
to eliminate
the awesome threat
of nuclear catastrophe
and environmental ruin.

Be informed,
hopeful
and energetic.

Be vigilant
with your thoughts
of peace and love.

Sense your power
to lift
the mood of despair.

Let your enthusiasm
seep in
and penetrate
the collective consciousness!

M eet with people,
talk with people,
share with people.

Find and support organizations
that channel our energy
into survival.

Write to your senators
and representatives
and other politicians.

Let them know
what you want them
to do.*

*John Kenneth Galbraith of Harvard University, at the
October 31, 1981 symposium of the Physicians for Social
Responsibility, told the 2,700 participants, "Nothing is
more needed in Washington than a rebuke to those who
are not pressing actively and energetically for arms
control." You can get the voting records of congressmen
on specific issues by writing the U.S. Senate, Capitol
Building, Washington, D.C. 20510 and the U.S. House of
Representatives, Capitol Building, Washington, D.C. 20515.

Most of the things
you are now doing
in your life
will become meaningless
or nonexistent
if we are hit
by nuclear catastrophe!

Take a new look
at your priorities . . . .

NUCLEAR
WAR
IS BAD FOR
SENATORS

This does not
necessarily mean
leaving your work
or your present lifestyle.

It means giving
an increasing energy
and priority
to expanding your own awareness,
to communicating with other people
who are now asleep,
and to withdrawing energy
from all thoughts and actions
which create human alienation,
separateness, destruction
and death.*

*Green ribbons were worn as a reminder of the children
being killed in Atlanta. Yellow ribbons were worn as a
reminder that our citizens were being held as hostages in
Iran. There is a worldwide energy to wear blue ribbons
symbolizing that everyone on earth is a hostage to the ever-
present threat of nuclear annihilation. You may wish to
buy a roll of ⅜" blue ribbon and a package of safety pins
and pass out these symbols of protest to your friends—
and wear one yourself. Thousands of people in Europe
are wearing leaves as Friends of the *Peace Book* by
Bernard Benson.

D̲o not wait
until others around you
are opening their hearts.

Instead,
begin doing things now
that are so desperately needed
for the conscious unfolding
of your life—
and the survival
of our species.

Your dedication
to saving our lives
and the planet Earth
will bring your own life
to a level of
satisfaction and well-being
that you may never
otherwise achieve.

You will become
increasingly happier
as you learn to love more.

And you will begin to discover
the miracle
of your full potential
as a human being.

Your life
will gain meaning
and purpose.

Your energy
can tip the scales
when you add it
to thousands of others'—
merging,
slowly raising
our collective consciousness
to the point of power
when it makes
the all-important difference!

This survival energy spreads
far beyond those involved
and touches every life
on Earth!

The change in you
is already taking place!

YOU NOW KNOW
THE IMMENSITY
OF THE DANGERS,
THE FUTILITY
OF SAFETY MEASURES,
AND THE NEED
FOR ACTION RIGHT NOW
USING THE POWER
OF OUR NEW AWARENESS.

The Hundredth Monkey Phenomenon
points out our responsibility
and our power.

It is up to every one of us
to change
the myths that say
we have to depend
on nuclear energy
for power and defense.

We can no longer believe
that the safeguards are adequate—
or that we are helpless
to change the national policies
of the governments
of our world.

We will replace the myths
with knowledge.

Our persistence
will relentlessly channel
our positive thoughts
toward peace
and a harmonizing world.

And that starts
right here—
in my heart and yours—
right now!

In this short book
I can only
give you a glimpse
of the miracle of life
you can experience . . . .

This rapture of life
is your birthright
to create and enjoy.

This book can only hope
to inspire you
to take the next steps
in your own development—
for your sake
and the survival
of our species.

NUCLEAR
WAR
IS BAD FOR
HOMO
SAPIENS

This is the
most pressing problem
we face today.

Everything else
in our civilization
is of secondary significance.

It is worthy
of your full attention
as an intelligent,
caring,
wise and
wonderful person.

We can begin to lose
the game of life
when we play
nuclear war games.

NUCLEAR
WAR
IS BAD FOR
HUMAN
POTENTIAL

Like children
our egos and minds
create the illusion
that the ideas in our heads
and our desires for "marbles"
are more important
than feelings
of human togetherness
in our hearts.

We cannot afford
to play such enthusiastic games
with loaded nuclear pistols
any more!

THE MARBLES JUST AREN'T WORTH IT!

APPENDIX

Increasing Awareness on Earth by Continuing Your Growth

There is no
one way to do it,
but you've got to do it
one way or another.

I'm devoting my life
to sharing ways
that I've learned
that help me
create inner peace
and emotional acceptance
and appreciation
of others.

I spend my full time
setting up teaching centers
and writing books.

I offer this loving energy
to the world
without accepting
any royalties or salary.

To get started
in creating
a new awareness
that will enrich your life
as well as helping our species
to survive the challenges
it now faces,
you may find
two of my books
particularly helpful:

Prescriptions for Happiness ($2.00)

*How to Enjoy Your Life
in Spite of It All* ($4.95)*

*Both of these books may be obtained through bookstores
or from Vision Books, 790 Commercial Avenue, Coos
Bay, Oregon 97420. Enclose the price plus $1.00 per book
for mailing.

These books
give you a blueprint
for becoming the master
of your mind—
and of your life.

They show you how to take
an enormous step
in piercing the illusions
of the separate-self
and discovering in you
the beauty,
wonder
and effectiveness
of the unified-self.

The loving and caring principles
in these books
are taught and lived
at a nonprofit training center
named ClearMind Trainings,
in Coos Bay, Oregon.

There you will find
helpful workshops
for opening your heart
and learning
to appreciate and love yourself—
and all others.

The Center also presents
weekend workshops
in various cities
throughout the nation.

To get more information
or a free catalog,
you can
write or phone:

ClearMind Trainings
790 Commercial Avenue
Coos Bay, Oregon 97420
(503) 267-6412

Your tax-exempt donation
will be used
to distribute free copies
of this book.

The author guarantees
that not one penny
will be wasted
or spent unnecessarily.

A monthly donation
of 10% of your income
could help us create
a safer world.

If we have
enough contributions,
we will send this book
to millions
throughout the world.*

*Checks may be made payable to The Vision Foundation,
   Inc., 790 Commercial Avenue, Coos Bay, Oregon 97420.

SHARE YOUR CONCERN

In responding to the urgent need to channel energy into our survival, you may wish to send this book to friends, groups and organizations here and abroad, and to representatives and officials on local, state and federal levels. Send only $2.00 per book and we'll pay the cost of mailing anywhere in the world!

Enclosed is $ _____ for _____ copies of
The Hundredth Monkey:

PLEASE PRINT

To: _____   To: _____

_____   _____

_____   _____
       (zip)   (zip)

To: _____   To: _____

_____   _____

_____   _____
       (zip)   (zip)

To: _____   From: _____
                                           (optional)

_____   _____

_____   _____
       (zip)   (zip)

**VISION BOOKS, 790 Commercial Avenue,
Coos Bay, Oregon 97420**
Your energy may make the difference!

loving more

World
Peace

demanding less

MANY THANKS TO
Britta Zetterberg
and Penny Hannig
for their wealth of
helpful suggestions
for improving this book.
Cover design by
Sharon Steere.